Y0-BRR-950

CAREERS IN HEALTHCARE

Occupational Therapists

Careers in Healthcare

Athletic Trainers
Clinical & Medical Laboratory Scientists
Dental Hygienists
Dietitian & Nutritionists
EMTs & Paramedics
Nurses
Occupational Therapists
Orthotists & Prosthetists
Physical Therapists
Physician Assistants
Respiratory Therapists
Speech Pathologists & Audiologists
Ultrasound Technicians

CAREERS IN
HEALTHCARE

Occupational Therapists

Jennifer Hunsaker

MASON CREST
PHILADELPHIA

Mason Crest
450 Parkway Drive, Suite D
Broomall, PA 19008
www.masoncrest.com

©2018 by Mason Crest, an imprint of National Highlights, Inc.

Printed and bound in the United States of America.

CPSIA Compliance Information: Batch #CHC2017.
For further information, contact Mason Crest at 1-866-MCP-Book.

First printing
1 3 5 7 9 8 6 4 2

Library of Congress Cataloging-in-Publication Data

on file at the Library of Congress
ISBN: 978-1-4222-3801-1 (hc)
ISBN: 978-1-4222-7989-2 (ebook)

Careers in Healthcare series ISBN: 978-1-4222-3794-6

QR CODES AND LINKS TO THIRD-PARTY CONTENT

Table of Contents

KEY ICONS TO LOOK FOR:

Words to understand: These words with their easy-to-understand definitions will increase the reader's understanding of the text while building vocabulary skills.

Sidebars: This boxed material within the main text allows readers to build knowledge, gain insights, explore possibilities, and broaden their perspectives by weaving together additional information to provide realistic and holistic perspectives.

Educational Videos: Readers can view videos by scanning our QR codes, providing them with additional educational content to supplement the text. Examples include news coverage, moments in history, speeches, iconic sports moments and much more!

Text-dependent questions: These questions send the reader back to the text for more careful attention to the evidence presented there.

Research projects: Readers are pointed toward areas of further inquiry connected to each chapter. Suggestions are provided for projects that encourage deeper research and analysis.

Series glossary of key terms: This back-of-the book glossary contains terminology used throughout this series. Words found here increase the reader's ability to read and comprehend higher-level books and articles in this field.

Occupational therapists are concerned with a person's "occupations," or the things that they do that occupy their time.

 Words to Understand in This Chapter

accommodating—fitting the needs of an individual.

dexterity—skill in performing tasks, especially with the hands.

mobility—the ability to move in a way that is appropriate.

sensory—pertaining to the bodily senses—sight, smell, taste, touch, and hearing.

sensory processing disorder—a condition where the brain has trouble receiving and processing information received from the senses.

What Do Occupational Therapists Do?

Emily was in a horrific car accident when she was 20 years old. Her car was hit by a speeding tractor-trailer. While it was miraculous that she survived at all, she quickly discovered that her traumatic brain injury required her to learn how to walk again with the help of a physical therapist. What she didn't anticipate was that her injury would also cause her to lose the *dexterity* she once had in her hands. She set about working with an occupational therapist (OT) to relearn how to write, type, cook, and otherwise take care of herself.

What Is Occupational Therapy?

Occupational therapy is the process of helping patients develop, recover, or improve their skills for everyday living. Those who are ill or who have been injured or disabled receive occupational therapy to help them live as independently as possible while *accommodating* for their limitations. Ultimately, occupational therapy is designed to help people be successful in daily living.

Children's primary "occupation" is learning and playing with their peers. Occupational therapy may help them develop their core strength through climbing, jumping, or swinging. In children who cannot write, that may be developing fine motor skills through coloring, drawing, painting, or even picking up items and placing them in bins.

We take our ability to do daily tasks for granted until we are faced with the challenge of an injury, accident, illness, or disability.

Occupational therapy for adults helps them become more independent. Therapy might focus on performing daily tasks, such as getting dressed, driving a car, typing on a computer, or cooking simple meals.

The Occupational Therapy Process

EVALUATION: Once a person has been identified as requiring occupational therapy, she is referred to a qualified, certified occupational therapist. The occupational therapist then performs a series of evaluations to determine the extent of the patient's skills at this point. Not only does this process give the occupational therapist a baseline for evaluating the patient's progress, the therapist is also able to see exactly what problems need to be addressed. The evaluation process includes taking a detailed patient history, discussing the patient's current challenges and needs, and reviewing referral materials from the doctor or other health care provider. The

Educational Video

Scan here to get an up-close look at a day in the life of an occupational therapist:

OT may ask the patient to attempt to perform some of the tasks she is struggling with to see exactly how to accommodate the patient and treat the issue(s). The patient may also be asked to perform seemingly unrelated tasks to pinpoint any underlying problems that prevent her from completing the task in question.

A Patient I Will Never Forget

Ruth Walton, an occupational therapist working in a large city, recalls one of her most memorable patients.

"I didn't realize how much creativity it would take to provide therapy to some clients. I remember one little girl with cerebral palsy who came to me completely dependent on her parents to dress her, feed her, bathe her, and take care of her. We worked for several months trying to help her gain the dexterity she needed to perform simple tasks, like brushing her hair or brushing her teeth, and she just wasn't getting it. You could tell she was frustrated by the whole process and I couldn't help but feel bad that we weren't getting anywhere.

Finally, it occurred to me that she needed larger handles on her toothbrush and hairbrush. I went home and wrapped duct tape around a brand new toothbrush until it created a wider handle for her to grip. Suddenly, all the therapy we had been doing clicked for her. I will never forget how it felt to watch her wrap her little hand around the toothbrush and begin brushing her teeth. She wasn't perfect at it, but in that moment she had a glimpse of what we were trying to accomplish. She took off after that.

That experience drove home to me the idea that OT is a balance between teaching someone how to function in her environment and creating accommodations in her environment for her limitations."

INTERVENTION: Once the patient has been evaluated, therapy (or intervention) can begin. Occupational therapy takes a tremendous amount of creativity. To simulate daily living tasks in a way that is fun and engaging, OTs look for activities that call for the use of similar areas of the body without seeming like therapy. For instance, a child who struggles with using his left hand might be given an activity where he takes turns with his left and right hands to see how far he can throw a softball. To the child, it seems like a game but he is actually strengthening his arms, hands, and core muscles as part of the therapeutic process.

Therapeutic intervention can last a few weeks for someone with an injury or several months or even years for someone

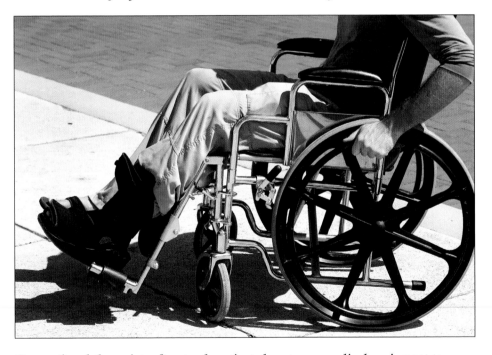

Occupational therapists often teach patients how to use medical equipment to improve their mobility.

People who have experienced an illness or accident often see dramatic changes in their life.

with a severe disability. Throughout the process, it is important for the OT to remain positive and upbeat. The patient is likely to experience frustration at not being able to progress as quickly as she would like. It is the OT's job to help her recognize the progress she is making.

MEASURING OUTCOMES: At the end of each session, the OT charts the patient's progress and makes notes about the day's session. This serves two purposes. First, the OT is able to keep track of the progress of multiple patients throughout the day. Second, it allows the OT to evaluate each patient's needs and make adjustments for the next therapy session.

Periodically, the OT will conduct a reevaluation to assess how far the patient has come in therapy. The patient is able to see his progress, but more importantly the OT is able to measure the therapy's outcome and either recommend additional therapy or discharge the patient from her care.

The process of charting and documentation is also important when dealing with insurance companies. While many insurance companies cover occupational therapy, they require documentation from time to time that therapy is still a necessary part of the patient's recovery.

Occupational Therapy and the Senses

Occupational therapists also work with children and adults who have difficulty integrating information from their senses into their daily lives. Our brains process enormous amounts of *sensory* information on a regular basis. We sense movement through our inner ear system, we smell, taste, touch, and hear, and we experience textures when we eat, dress, shower, or even sleep. For children and adults who have a *sensory processing disorder*, simple processes such as eating become difficult because the brain cannot easily process texture information and overreacts to stimulation. Occupational therapists are trained to help their patients identify problems with sensory input and use strategies to incorporate that information in simple and easy ways.

Developing hand-eye coordination in children with disabilities is an important part of occupational therapy.

Occupational Therapy versus Physical Therapy

Occupational therapy primarily focuses on the patient's ability to live independently. This encompasses all the activities of daily life, including bathing, dressing, grooming and hygiene, and working. Occupational therapists also come up with ways to make accommodations for any physical disabilities or difficulties patients have. If you are unable to reach your hands above your head to get dressed, for instance, an occupational therapist will teach you ways to accommodate this difficulty while working on improving your range of motion and your ability to dress yourself.

By contrast, physical therapy is chiefly concerned with a patient's *mobility*, strength, and overall agility. Physical therapists may work on a patient's core strength so he can sit, stand, crawl, walk, or run. They may also address a person's ability to position his body to accomplish all the mobility tasks required of him.

 Text-Dependent Questions

1. What are some "occupations" in children that can be addressed through occupational therapy?
2. How do occupational therapy and physical therapy differ from each other? How are they similar?
3. What role do evaluation, treatment, and measuring outcomes play in the occupational therapy process?

 Research Project

Make a list of all of the things, big or small, that you do in a single day. From reading a book to doing homework, list all the daily tasks you usually perform. Then, imagine trying to do each of those tasks with one hand tied behind your back. How would the way you accomplish those things change? What ways would you need to accommodate not having the use of one hand?

From holding a pencil to climbing on a playground, many occupational therapists work with children with disabilities.

Words to Understand in This Chapter

acute care—a branch of health care where the patient receives short-term, focused treatment in response to an injury, illness, or surgery.

holistic—referring to treatment of the whole person and not just one particular part.

inpatient—referring to medical treatment done while the patient is staying in a hospital, rehabilitation center, or nursing home.

outpatient—referring to medical treatment done without the patient being admitted to the hospital or other health care facility.

reasonable accommodations—changes made to a job or workplace that help an employee do a job despite having a disability.

A Look at the Opportunities

O ccupational therapy is one of the fastest-growing occupations in the country. According to the U.S. Department of Labor's Bureau of Labor Statistics, the ranks of occupational therapists are expected to grow by 27 percent over the next decade. This is much faster than all other professions. With more than 110,000 occupational therapy jobs currently in the United States, there is expected to be an increase of nearly 30,000 jobs in the next ten years.

About half of all OTs work in hospitals or clinics. The rest work in nursing homes, schools, rehabilitation centers, or in the homes of their patients. Occupational therapy plays an important part in the treatment of Alzheimer's disease, autism spectrum disorder, and cerebral palsy, as well as the treatment of injuries resulting in the loss of function or the loss of a limb.

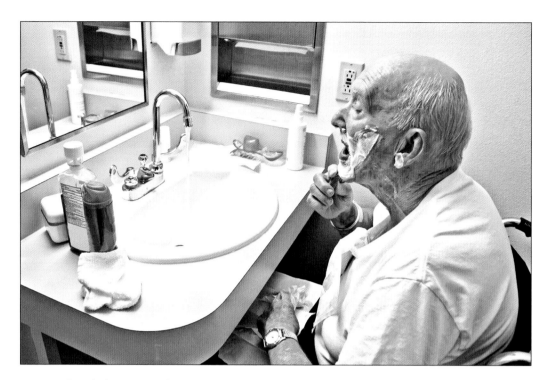

Occupational therapists who work in hospitals focus on ways to help patients live safely at home.

Because of the nature of their job, OTs are required to spend the majority of their time being physically active. They may be required to lift, hold, walk, climb, run, or jump during the course of therapy.

Occupational Therapy in the Hospital

Any time patients are in the hospital for a severe medical condition, they are receiving *acute care*. The primary goal of acute care is to restore their function as quickly as possible and return them to their home or a long-term care facility.

According to the American Occupational Therapy Association, the occupational therapist offers a *holistic* approach to a patient's initial recovery. While many specialists focus on their individual role in the patient's care, OTs are able to see how all those processes dovetail with one another and how the patient will need to be accommodated while he is recovering.

For instance, an orthopedic surgeon is concerned with operating on the bones, muscles, and nerves in a person's hand; a physical therapist works to restore strength and mobility in the patient's finger and wrist joints; and a nurse focuses attention on how a wound is healing. The OT sees how all of these combine to result in how the person will use her hand in the future as well as how she will compensate for her lack of use right now.

OTs are trained in human anatomy and physiology and, in a hospital setting, they become

Educational Video

For a video showing how OTs help veterans, scan here

familiar with the surgical process, ways the area should be wrapped or splinted to preserve the joint's function, and ways to keep the skin intact and to promote healing during the entire recovery process. They may perform bedside evaluations relating to eating and swallowing to see if the patient is capable of eating solid foods. They may recommend dietary accommodations to compensate for any problems the patient may have in chewing or swallowing. OTs may give patients training in how to care for themselves with the help of medical equipment or devices. They may train patients in how to deal with post-surgical weakness or healing requirements. They may also train family members in ways to help patients once they return home so they do not end up in the hospital or clinic again.

Occupational Therapy in a Clinic

Outpatient occupational therapy clinics have a different approach than hospitals. Rather than looking for ways to quickly teach patients and caregivers how to function outside the hospital, outpatient clinics focus on the continuing care of patients who need occupational therapy. OTs who work in a clinic often have therapy areas that mimic natural settings. For those working with adults, they may have a kitchen where patients can work on the skills they need to cook a simple meal. For those working with children, the therapy room may look a lot like a playground or an obstacle course where young patients can run, jump, climb, or swing. In a clinic setting, OTs set short-term and long-term goals for the patient's progress. They then periodically evaluate their patient's progress toward those goals and set new ones.

Occupational Therapy in Skilled Nursing Facilities

Skilled nursing facilities are *inpatient* rehabilitation centers and nursing homes where patients who are unable to care for themselves receive medical care and therapy. The main difference between outpatient clinics and skilled nursing facilities is

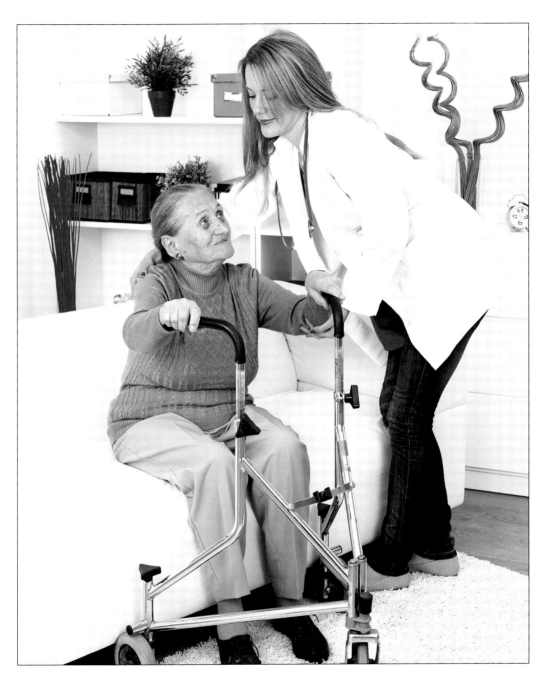

Home health occupational therapists work with patients in their own homes to make sure they can do the things they want to do, safely.

that patients live where they receive therapy, either on a short-term basis (rehab centers) or a permanent basis (nursing homes). In general, those who are living in a skilled nursing facility are older or have severe mental or physical disabilities that keep them from living independently. OTs who work in rehabilitation centers have a major impact on how quickly their patients can return home. In fact, studies have shown that patients who receive high-intensity occupational therapy in a

Occupational therapists often work with patients in skilled nursing facilities and rehabilitation centers to help them regain or preserve their independence.

rehabilitation center have a shorter length of stay than those who do not.

In a skilled nursing facility, OTs work with patients, caregivers, and other health care providers to identify the ways patients are limited and how those limitations keep them from performing their daily occupational activities. The OT also works with the health care team to prepare the patient for discharge and address any accommodations they will need at home. When discharge is not possible, the OT will document a patient's loss of function and make recommendations for his continued care.

Occupational Therapy in the Schools

School districts throughout the country employ OTs to work with children in an educational setting. Since they are concerned with every occupation a person performs, OTs can help children who are limited by the school environment or who have difficulty participating in the educational process. This may mean teaching children with fine-motor difficulties how to hold a pencil, helping kids who have sensory processing disorders learn how to deal with noisy environments, or developing alternative methods of teaching a child with disabilities.

Occupational therapy services are determined by an Individualized Educational Plan (IEP), a document that is created in response to a child's physical, mental, or learning disability. The OT must keep extensive records of the child's progress in order to continue offering therapy. OTs in educational settings may serve one or more schools at a time, requiring them to travel within the school district.

Occupational Therapy at Home

Even those who cannot safely leave their home may require occupational therapy. About 9 percent of all occupational therapists offer home health services. Here, the OT uses the patient's home environment and a few portable tools to help her regain her independence. While occupational therapy in general requires a tremendous amount of creativity, performing it in different environments every day is the true test of an OT's ability to adapt.

In a home health care environment, the OT's first goal is to ensure the safety of the patient. This may mean recommending accommodations to prevent the patient from falling or becoming injured while performing daily tasks. Once any issues threatening the patient's safety have been addressed, the OT can then evaluate the patient's current level of functioning and begin teaching her how to do the things she wants to do. While the majority of patients who receive home health services are older adults, many OTs prefer to work in the homes of children with disabilities to teach their caregivers how to perform therapy when the OT is not there.

Did You Know?

Hospitals employ the largest percentage of occupational therapists at 27 percent. Outpatient clinics are not far behind, employing 24 percent of all occupational therapists.

Occupational Therapy in Other Settings

While the majority of OTs work directly with patients in a clinical setting, some OTs are hired by companies to make *reasonable accommodations* for their workers. The Americans with Disabilities Act requires businesses to make reasonable accommodations for employees with disabilities to work there. It also requires businesses to have adequate accessibility for those who have disabilities. Since OTs are experts at creating accommodations for people who have physical and mental limitations, they are ideal consultants for businesses who wish to comply with the Americans with Disabilities Act.

 ## Text-Dependent Questions

1. How do the goals of an OT who works in a hospital differ from those of an OT who works in an outpatient clinic?
2. What services does an OT who works in an educational setting provide?
3. What can OTs contribute to businesses?

 ## Research Project

Make an appointment to speak with an occupational therapist who works in an area you might be interested in. Ask him about his favorite part of the job as well as the most challenging part. Find out if he has interests or experiences in other settings. Ask why he chose this particular area of focus.

The clinical internship is an important part of an occupational therapist's education.

 Words to Understand in This Chapter

accredited—officially authorized to provide education.

contact hours—number of hours an OT is required to receive direct instruction in a classroom setting.

continuing education—post-degree classes, courses, seminars, or workshops designed to help OTs remain current in the latest developments in the profession.

licensure—the verification, provided by a state, that a person is able to perform a particular job.

neuroanatomy—the study of the structures and functions of the brain.

Education
and Training

Becoming an occupational therapist takes a great deal of time, but can result in a rewarding, in-demand career. An OT must obtain a master's degree or higher, and the *licensure* process is divided into five steps: (1) undergraduate education, (2) graduate education, (3) clinical internships, (4) passing the National Board for Certification of Occupational Therapists (NBCOT) exam, and (5) state licensure.

1. Undergraduate Education

To become an occupational therapist, you will need to get at least a master's degree. Before you can begin your OT education, you will first need to obtain a bachelor's degree. Many OT programs require students seeking admission to take classes in

According to a recent study, 13 percent of all children in the public school system receive services for disabilities.

biology, anatomy and physiology, kinesiology, and psychology. Many people choose to study exercise science or physiology, psychology, or another health science–related field. As you are finishing your bachelor's degree, you will take a graduate entrance exam and begin applying to graduate programs.

2. Graduate Education

In deciding on a master's degree program, it is important to look for a university with an *accredited* occupational therapy program. This means the university has met the standards for educating potential OTs, specified by the American

Occupational Therapy Association. For a complete list of accredited programs, visit www.aota.org. Only students who have graduated from an accredited program of study are allowed to take the board examination to become a licensed OT.

Typically, occupational therapy classwork takes two years, with an additional yearlong clinical internship and several clinical experiences interspersed throughout the student's education. Classes may include *neuroanatomy* and physiology, therapy techniques, the history of the profession, and evaluation in occupational therapy. Occupational therapy students are given chances to observe OTs in action as well as opportunities to assist licensed OTs in actual clinical settings. When considering a graduate program, be sure to ask the following questions:

- How many students apply to the program each year? How many are accepted?
- What is the first-time pass rate on the NBCOT exam?
- How much does tuition cost, and are there scholarships or student loans available to help offset the cost?
- Are students allowed to work at a job during their education? Does the graduate program offer a work-study track?
- What are the qualifications of the typical student who is admitted to the program?

One important distinction should be made between entry-level master's programs and doctoral programs in occupational therapy. You can complete a master's degree program from an accredited university to sit for the NBCOT examination and become a licensed OT. Doctoral programs require more classes before being admitted, an additional clinical internship, and a culminating project. Graduates of doctoral programs are still required to sit for the NBCOT exam before beginning their practice, but they are referred to as "Doctor" when they are finished.

3. Clinical Internships

Before students can obtain a graduate degree, they must first complete one or more clinical internships. At the very least, internships must be 16 weeks long and place students in a situation where they intend to practice. Under the supervision of a certified OT, students are allowed to conduct therapy with a variety of clients. Not only does this enable them to draw connections between classroom learning and the real world, but they can see a variety of environments where they may wish to practice. While one 16-week clinical internship is required for certification, many programs require more than one so students have a chance to practice in a variety of clinical settings.

4. Passing the NBCOT Exam

Once you have received your master's or doctoral degree, you can take the National Board for Certification of Occupational Therapy exam. The NBCOT is a not-for-profit credentialing agency that ensures that those becoming OTs have the knowledge and skills necessary to succeed. The exam itself is a 200-question, multiple-choice test with a four-hour time limit. While the idea of being tested on three years' worth of knowl-

To many people, what an occupational therapist does looks a lot like play.

edge is daunting to some, most accredited universities have programs designed to prepare you for the test. If you study in class and do well there, you will likely pass the NBCOT exam.

5. State Licensure

Each state in the United States has different requirements for issuing a license to perform occupational therapy. For those who have recently passed the NBCOT exam, licensure is as often as simple as paying a fee to the state's licensing agency. OTs need to obtain a license from each state where they plan

During their internships, OTs learn how to use different materials to achieve an end result.

to practice. If they move to another state, they will need to comply with the new state's licensing requirements before they are allowed to practice there. Each state has a different length of time the license to practice is valid before the OT must apply for license renewal.

Continuing Education

To renew their license to practice, an OT must fulfill *continuing education* requirements. Continuing education occurs after your initial education is over; hence the term continuing. It consists of classes, seminars, workshops, and conferences designed to help OTs remain up-to-date on all the latest developments in occupational therapy. While many OTs willingly participate in continuing education classes, they cannot renew their license to practice in most states without it. Some states require a certain number of continuing education units (CEUs) while others require something called *contact hours*. Contact hours are the number of hours OTs must spend in the classroom before they can apply for relicensing. In most cases, ten contact hours are equal to one CEU.

What You Can Do Now

Becoming an occupational therapist is a rigorous process. The best way to prepare for the intensity of the coursework and the clinical environment is to begin to learn about the human body right now. High school science classes, such as biology, chemistry, human anatomy, and physiology, will help you become familiar with the body, the way it moves, and how things can go wrong. Classes in psychology and health will prepare you to study the human mind and how it reacts when it is challenged over the course of therapy. You will also learn about a person's normal development, which will help you understand the mental and physical challenges facing people with disabilities. Advanced

Educational Video

Scan here for some career advice from OT students:

Occupational Therapy Assistants

Occupational therapy assistants (OTAs) provide many of the same day-to-day therapies an OT does, but do them under the direction of an occupational therapist. To meet the demands on them, OTs often work closely with OTAs to treat as many patients as possible. To become an OTA, you will need to complete an associate's degree from an accredited program. This will include two years of classes focused on biology, anatomy, and kinesiology, and will include a minimum of 16 hours of clinical experience, where you can try your newly acquired skills on actual patients.

Nearly all states require OTAs to be licensed or certified. Licensure nearly always requires candidates to pass the National Board for Certification of Occupational Therapists exam. In most states, they must also take periodic continuing education to keep their license. While many OTAs go on to become OTs, many find satisfaction in their job as it is. On average, OTAs make $54,520 per year, with the majority of them working in OT offices.

math classes will make college-level math much easier.

It is also critical to learn about your own health and how to maintain it. Occupational therapy is a physically demanding job. Regardless of where you practice, you will be required to lift, bend, stretch, walk, and climb. You need to maintain your own physical health and fitness to be able to help others. Develop good nutrition, exercise, and sleep habits now while you are young. Not only will these serve you well in your professional life, you will be better able to handle the stress of college and the workplace.

 Text-Dependent Questions

1. What are the five steps required to become an occupational therapist?
2. What should you look for in an occupational therapy program?
3. What role does continuing education play in the development of a successful OT?

 Research Project

Begin looking at accredited occupational therapy programs in your area. Find out the following for each one:

- Where the program is located
- How many people applied last year and how many were admitted
- What the first-time pass rate is on the NCBOT exam
- How much tuition costs
- What undergraduate program is required for admission to the master's degree program
- How students feel about attending the school, including campus recreation and community service opportunities.

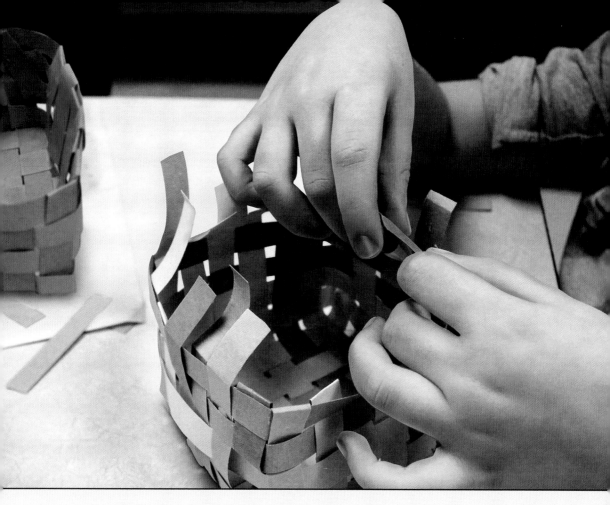

Arts and crafts therapy was used as early as the 1800s to treat patients in asylums. Today it is an important part of occupational therapy.

 Words to Understand in This Chapter

mental hygienists—a term referring to adherents of the mental hygiene movement in the early 20th century.

moral treatment movement—a movement in the late 1700s that was based on the idea that the mentally and physically disabled should be treated with compassion, rather than being shunted away in institutions.

neurasthenia—a condition characterized by chronic fatigue, general lack of energy, and an inability to sustain energy while performing a task.

occupation—in the OT profession, a term that refers to any way people choose to spend their time.

The Evolution of Occupational Therapy

The profession of occupational therapist is one of the fastest-growing fields in the United States. Estimated to grow by 27 percent in the next ten years, occupational therapy offers assistance to people who are struggling to perform their *occupation*.

While many people think of an occupation as a job, OTs define it as any activity that occupies a portion of a person's time. The occupation of older adults, for instance, may be taking care of their own physical needs, such as showering, dressing, grooming, going to the bathroom, preparing meals, and doing household chores. Young children's occupation may be playing, learning, and interacting with others in appropriate ways.

There are more than 110,000 current occupational therapy jobs in the United States. That number is expected to increase

While many children receive occupational therapy in schools today, they also receive therapy in outpatient clinics around the country.

by more than 30,000 jobs in the next decade, making it one of the occupations in the greatest demand in the country.

Salary

As of May 2015, occupational therapists made an average of $80,150 a year. The lowest-paid OTs earned less than $53,250, while the highest-paid OTs earned more than $116,000. On average, the highest-paid OTs tend to work in skilled nursing facilities, such as nursing homes and rehabilitation centers. There, OTs earn an average of $89,000. OTs who work for home health care companies earn an average of $88,000, with those working in an outpatient clinic making an average of about $82,600. Hospitals have the highest concentration of OTs, and those who work in hospitals are paid an average of about $80,250. Rounding out the salary list are school districts, where OTs make an average of about $69,500.

Early Occupational Therapy

Before the words occupational and therapy ever came together to form the profession we know today as occupational therapy, a movement that began in the early 1800s, known as the *moral treatment movement* called for all patients to be treated with dignity and respect. Its prime mover, Philippe Pinel, took over an insane asylum after the French Revolution and was the first person to use "organized programs of activity and occupation" to treat patients. Up to that point, most people placed in insane asylums were not insane; rather, they were physically or mentally disabled.

Around the same time, an Englishman named William Tuke founded a place in Yorkshire, England called the York Retreat. He, too, began to use the moral treatment approach in treating patients believed to be insane with activities and what has come to be called occupational therapies, rather than medication and isolation. Simultaneously, in the United States, Doctor Benjamin Rush began implementing the same types of treatment, reinforcing the belief that establishing a structure and giving patients simple work tasks led to better health.

From 1880 to 1910, the arts and crafts movement swept the United States. As a reaction to the industrial revolution, many people clung to the belief that making something with their

Did You Know?

Benjamin Rush, one of the founders of occupational therapy, was a signer of the Declaration of Independence. He is also known as the "Father of American Psychiatry."

own two hands was healthier than allowing a machine to do the work for them. Rooted in this movement, Dr. Herbert Hall began using arts and crafts in the treatment of patients with hysteria and a condition called *neurasthenia*, or chronic fatigue syndrome. His pottery, basket making, and carpentry workshop gave rise to the belief that chronic conditions could be alleviated by manual occupation.

The term occupational therapy was coined by a man named George Edward Barton. After enduring paralysis, tuberculosis, and a foot amputation, he determined that manual occupations could help a person feel better about himself. He later opened a workshop called Consolation House in upstate New York, where the National Society for the Promotion of Occupational Therapy was formed on March 15, 1917. As a result, the profession of occupational therapy was created.

Eleanor Clarke Slagle attended that founding meeting of the National Society and became known as the "Mother of Occupational Therapy." At the time, the "mental hygiene movement" was just beginning to take hold. Instead of focusing on mental illness, so-called *mental hygienists* used preventive measures and early interventions to prevent the progression of mental illness symptoms. Eleanor Clarke Slagle was a social worker who took a class in curative occupation and found her calling in life. She was a staunch supporter of "habit

The Individuals with Disabilities Education Act guaranteed that children with disabilities would be given the tools they need to attend school.

training," a process involving replacing bad habits with new, positive ones.

War Propels the Profession

In 1917, the same year as the famous Consolation House meeting, the United States entered World War I. As is the case in all wars, thousands of injured service members came home requiring a new set of therapeutic techniques so they could perform everyday tasks. At Walter Reed Hospital in Washington, D.C., nurses were trained to be "reconstruction aides." These reconstruction aides taught injured service members how to work

Educational Video

For a look at how occupational therapy and physical therapy are different, scan here:

with wood and metal, build toys, weave, and do block printing as a part of their rehabilitation. The idea that activity could be therapeutic was suddenly validated on a national level.

In 1918, Congress passed the Soldier's Rehabilitation Act, giving occupational therapy the federal government's imprimatur for the treatment of service members in hospitals around the country. On the heels of this act came the Civilian Vocational Rehabilitation Act, which authorized federal funding for similar services for non-service members. This level of growth continued until the Great Depression (1929–1939).

Upon the United States' entry into World War II in 1941, the demand for OTs skyrocketed. While there were a few OT schools still open, training took a minimum of 18 months and the demand was so critical that the military needed several

Did You Know?

In 1921, members of the National Society for the Promotion of Occupational Therapy voted to change the name of the professional organization to the American Occupational Therapy Association, the name the organization bears to this day. Regardless of the name change, the focus remains the same.

hundred OTs immediately. As a result, the military created an intensive 4-month course for the education of occupational therapists and the number of people in the profession rose more than 7000 percent.

Legislation

Since World War II, which ended in 1945, occupational therapy has been shaped primarily by legislation. With the introduction of each piece of legislation, occupational therapy became a more substantial and respected part of the health care team for children and adults with illnesses and disabilities. In 1963, the Community Mental Health Act led to a policy of deinstitutionalization for the mentally and physically disabled. Medicare became law in 1965. The Rehabilitation Act of 1973 ensured the civil rights of those with disabilities and made sure the most severely disabled receive services first.

 **Did You Know?**

The highest-paid occupational therapists can be found in Nevada, Texas, and New Jersey, respectively. The city with the highest-paid occupational therapists? Longview, Texas.

The Education for All Handicapped Children Act of 1975 mandated mainstream education for disabled children and designated occupational therapy as a service to be provided in the schools. The EAHC was then revised to create the Individuals with Disabilities Education Act (IDEA) in 1991, although the principle behind the law remains the same.

The Handicapped Children Protections Act of 1986 made intervention services available to ill and disabled children from birth, rather than forcing families to wait until the child was school-aged before receiving occupational therapy. The Technology-Related Assistance for Individuals with Disabilities Act of 1988 made assistive technology devices available to all individuals with disabilities. These devices are often used in occupational therapy to help patients communicate, move, or enjoy the activities of daily life.

Educational Video

For a short-review of the history of occupational therapy, scan here:

The Americans with Disabilities Act, passed in 1990, mandated that employers make reasonable accommodations for workers with disabilities. This meant that businesses could not refuse to hire people with disabilities if they were qualified for a particular job and could perform it with reasonable accommodations. It also meant that businesses would have to make accommodations in their buildings for those with physical disabilities. This law opened up a whole new avenue for occupational therapists—that of business consultants. Not only can OTs make recommendations for changes to a business's building that would accommodate those with disabilities, they can help set up reasonable accommodations for workers with disabilities as well.

Occupational Therapy Today

Despite recognition of the value of occupational therapy reflected in several laws currently on the books, there is a push in the profession to return to its roots, so to speak. Occupational therapists are advocating a more compassionate approach to care that characterized the moral treatment movement. Not only do today's OTs work to make sure all practitioners have the knowledge, skills, and abilities they need to provide excellent care, they hold to the belief that bodies and minds can be healed through occupation.

 Text-Dependent Questions

1. What occupational environment accounts for the highest concentration of OTs? Where does that environment rank in pay? Why do you suppose that is?
2. What role did war play in the development of the OT profession?
3. How did legislation shape the profession as we know it today?

 Research Project

Watch the educational videos in this chapter. Then, begin reading about the history of occupational therapy. If possible, talk to some people who received OT when they were very young. Ask them about the activities they performed as part of the OT regimen, and how those activities helped them recover from injury, illness, or disability.

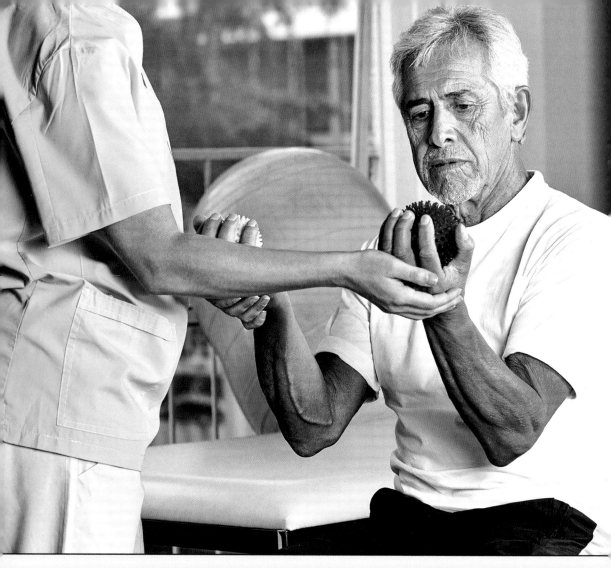

Being an occupational therapist takes a tremendous amount of creativity.

 Words to Understand in This Chapter

clinical supervisor—a licensed occupational therapist who oversees a clinical internship, making notes, giving feedback, and reporting to professors at the university.

ingenuity—cleverness, inventiveness.

Overview
and Interview

As a profession, occupational therapy is expected to grow much faster than the average of all other occupations in the next ten years. OTs possess a graduate degree, either a master's degree or a doctorate, and have completed an extensive clinical internship. They have passed the NBCOT exam and become licensed through the state where they will practice.

OTs have an extensive knowledge of the human body's processes and movements, and how to help people continue their desired occupations, or the ways in which they spend their time. More than half of all OTs work in a hospital or outpatient clinic while the highest-paid OTs can be found in skilled nursing facilities, such as nursing homes and rehabilitation centers. Research has linked occupational therapy to better overall health, faster recovery times, and greater social skills.

Occupational therapists and physical therapists often work together toward similar goals.

Q&A with a Professional in the Field

Ruth Walton

Ruth Walton, an occupational therapist in a large city, talks about her experiences as an occupational therapist in this one-on-one interview.

Question: How long have you been an occupational therapist?

Ruth: I actually started out as a chemist working for a pharmaceutical company. I did that for many years and finally decided to go back to school and become an occupational therapist. I graduated from the University of Utah in 2015 with a master's degree in occupational therapy and began working at a hospital nearby.

Question: What inspired you to get into this field?

Ruth: I have always been interested in the way the body works. As a pharmaceutical researcher, I was able to work on treatments for Alzheimer's disease and cancer, both very exciting areas of study. I wrote disclosures for patent applications and worked with other chemists and biologists to decide the direction for our studies. But it felt sort of distant from the patients we were trying to help. The further along in my career I got, the more I wanted to have that connection with patients. Finally, I quit my job, went back to school, and got my master's degree in occupational therapy.

Question: What kinds of classes did you take in your program of study?

Ruth: I originally thought that, since I had worked in drug research for so long, I would have a leg up on the rest of the students, and that would make up for the fact that I was so much older than most of them were. And while having a background in chemistry and drug research certainly didn't hurt, I was surprised that there was still so much to learn about the human body and the way it moved and worked. My coursework focused on evaluating patients' occupational therapy needs as well as methods for treating a variety of conditions.

Question: Where did you work when you first graduated?

Ruth: I did my clinical internship with the same hospital where I work now. It was such a positive experience for both myself and the department I was working in that they offered me a full-time position once I graduated. That actually happens quite frequently. Because occupational therapists are in such high demand, if occupational therapy students do well during their internship, they are often offered a job in that location once they finish.

Question: What surprised you the most when you first became an occupational therapist?

Ruth: There is a tremendous level of creativity that goes along with being an OT. Where I was in pharmaceuticals first, there was so much government regulation and so many

Daily tasks such as typing on the computer often must be re-taught to people who have experienced a traumatic brain injury.

An occupational therapist teaches a patient how to use her non-dominant hand to stir a pot.

internal protocols, there was no room for going off book and doing what you want. In occupational therapy you are constantly looking for creative ways to help patients learn how to compensate for their illnesses, injuries, or disabilities. It has definitely been the most fun part of my job. I work

Educational Video

Scan here for some questions to consider about the OT profession:

primarily in an inpatient rehabilitation setting, so my patients are people who have had surgery or an event such as a stroke, and they're anxious to get home and regain their independence. They are an extremely motivated bunch, which is great when you are doing therapy, but frustrating when you hit roadblocks. Creativity comes in handy when you hit those roadblocks because it helps them see that they can overcome their challenges with a little *ingenuity*.

Question: What has been the most challenging aspect of the job?

Ruth: The most challenging part was definitely getting through school. OT school is tough. It tests your mental abilities as well as your emotional toughness. But the professors aren't there to weed you out, they are there to help you succeed. When you recognize that you are all on the same team, it becomes easier to ask for help when you need it.

Question: What is the most rewarding aspect of the job?

Ruth: Discharging a patient from your care. While you develop relationships with these people, seeing them leave your care and return home is one of the best feelings. They are able to do what they want to do and be who they want to be without your help. Ultimately, we are there to work ourselves out of a job, one patient at a time.

Question: What role has technology played in your career?

Ruth: We do the majority of our patient charting on the computer. It's nice to be able to access a file from anywhere in the hospital without having to carry around a bunch of paper folders. OT also uses a variety of assistive technology devices to help patients communicate and perform daily tasks. These may be as complex as a communication board that tracks the eye movements of a patient then speaks for him or her or as simple as a board with several pictures on it that the patient can point to when he or she is in need of basic items.

We are also seeing tremendous advances in prosthetic limbs. Occupational therapy often focuses on helping those who have had amputations regain their independence. Someone with a prosthetic hand will need occupational therapy to relearn how to cook, shower, brush their teeth, or even type on a computer with their new prosthesis. The clumsy prostheses of ten years ago are becoming sleeker with more lifelike features that help the patient progress through OT more rapidly.

Question: What kind of personal traits do you think are important for an occupational therapist?

Ruth: Patience. OTs need a whole lot of patience. Whatever personal baggage you have needs to be left at the door. You have to put on a sunny disposition and work with your patients to help them do what they want to do. It is also important not to take their lack of enthusiasm too personally. Some people understand that you are there to help them and breeze through therapy every day with a smile on their face. Others are in pain or in denial about their condition and think there is nothing you can possibly do to help them. These are often the patients who, in the end, thank you the most for what you have done for them. But in the moment you sometimes find yourself biting your tongue and smiling.

It is important for an OT to have patience with her patients.

Question: What advice would you give new occupational therapists?

Ruth: Learn as much as you can from your clinical internship. That is a kind of grace period for new OTs. I understand the need to do well and impress your *clinical supervisor*, but ultimately you are there to ask questions, get advice, and try new things. Your supervisor does not expect you to know everything, so don't act like you do. Instead, the clinical internship is a time to put on your humble hat and ask for feedback that will make you a better OT.

Question: What advice would you give to someone who is considering a career in occupational therapy?

Ruth: Take as many science classes as you can. Graduate school will teach you the "how to" of the profession, but your undergraduate education can make grad school much easier if you take the required and suggested prerequisite classes. Take biology and chemistry. Take psychology and sociology. Take human anatomy and physiology. In fact, if you can take these classes while you are in high school, you can have a huge jump-start on other college students.

Question: Where do you see the profession in ten years?

Ruth: There is such a demand for high-quality OTs now, I can only see that demand increasing in the next decade. Occupational therapy assistants are also in demand. It would not surprise me if OTs take on a more managerial role where they assign OTAs to do the day-to-day clinical work. It would certainly mean OTs could take on more patients, but I think the majority of us would be sad at being a step removed from patient care. Most of us got into the profession to help people and seeing the look on their face when they finally make the connection between what you are asking them to do and how it will change their life makes it all worth it.

 Text-Dependent Questions

1. What does Ruth say are the most important characteristics for an occupational therapist to have?
2. What role does creativity play in occupational therapy?
3. Where does Ruth see the future of occupational therapy in the next ten years?

 Research Project

Find an occupational therapist in your area and ask her the same interview questions listed in this chapter. In what ways do her answers differ from Ruth's? In what ways are they the same? Did either interview make you want to practice in one particular area or another?

Series Glossary

accredited—a college or university program that has met all of the requirements put forth by the national organization for that job. The official stamp of approval for a degree.

Allied Health Professions—a group of professionals who use scientific principles to evaluate, diagnose and treat a variety of diseases. They also promote overall wellness and disease prevention in support of a variety of health care settings. (These may include physical therapists, dental hygienists, athletic trainers, audiologists, etc.)

American Medical Association (AMA)—the AMA is a professional group of physicians that publishes research about different areas of medicine. The AMA also advocates for its members to define medical concepts, professions, and recommendations.

anatomy—the study of the structure of living things; a person and/or animal's body.

associate's degree—a degree that is awarded to a student who has completed two years of study at a junior college, college, or university.

bachelor's degree—a degree that is awarded to a student by a college or university, usually after four years of study.

biology—the life processes especially of an organism or group.

chemistry—a science that deals with the composition, structure, and properties of substances and with the transformations that they undergo.

cardiology—the study of the heart and its action and diseases.

cardiopulmonary resuscitation (CPR)—a procedure designed to restore normal breathing after cardiac arrest that includes the clearance of air passages to the lungs, mouth-to-mouth method of artificial respiration, and heart massage by the exertion of pressure on the chest.

Centers for Disease Control—the Centers for Disease Control and Prevention (CDC) is a federal agency that conducts and supports health promotion, prevention and preparedness activities in the United States with the goal of improving overall public health.

diagnosis—to determine what is wrong with a patient. This process is especially important because it will determine the type of treatment the patient receives.

diagnostic testing—any tests performed to help determine a medical diagnosis.

EKG machine—an electrocardiogram (EKG or ECG) is a test that checks for problems with the electrical activity of your heart. An EKG shows the heart's electrical activity as line tracings on paper. The spikes and dips in the tracings are called waves. The heart is a muscular pump made up of four chambers.

first responder—the initial personnel who rush to the scene of an accident or an emergency.

Health Insurance Portability and Accountability Act (HIPAA)—a federal law enacted in 1996 that protects continuity of health coverage when a person changes or loses a job, that limits health-plan exclusions for preexisting medical conditions, that requires that patient medical information be kept private and secure, that standardizes electronic transactions involving health information, and that permits tax deduction of health insurance premiums by the self-employed.

internship—the position of a student or trainee who works in an organization, sometimes without pay, in order to gain work experience or satisfy requirements for a qualification.

kinesiology—the study of the principles of mechanics and anatomy in relation to human movement.

Master of Science degree—a Master of Science is a master's degree in the field of science awarded by universities in many countries, or a person holding such a degree.

obesity—a condition characterized by the excessive accumulation and storage of fat in the body.

pediatrics—the branch of medicine dealing with children.

physiology—a branch of biology that deals with the functions and activities of life or of living matter (as organs, tissues, or cells) and of the physical and chemical phenomena involved.

Surgeon General—the operational head of the US Public Health Department and the leading spokesperson for matters of public health.

Further Reading

Doidge, Norman. *The Brain That Changes Itself: Stories of Personal Triumph from the Frontiers of Brain Science.* New York: Viking, 2007.

Mason, Michael Paul. *Head Cases: Stories of Brain Injury and Its Aftermath.* New York: Farrar, Straus and Giroux, 2008.

Robison, John Elder. *Look Me in the Eye: My Life with Asperger's.* New York: Crown, 2007.

Sacks, Oliver. *On the Move: A Life.* New York: Vintage Books, a division of Penguin Random House, 2016.

Internet Resources

www.aota.org

The American Occupational Therapy Association (AOTA) is the national professional association established in 1917 to represent the interests and concerns of occupational therapy practitioners and students of occupational therapy and to improve the quality of occupational therapy services.

www.allthingsot.com/occupational-therapy

A collection of occupational therapy resources for students, practicing therapists, and anyone who is interested in learning more about the world of occupational therapy.

www.ada.gov

The Americans with Disabilities Act (ADA) became law in 1990. The ADA is a civil rights law that prohibits discrimination against individuals with disabilities in all areas of public life.

www.bls.gov/ooh/healthcare/athletic-trainers.htm

This government website provides information on salaries and job outlook for occupational therapists.

Publisher's Note: The websites listed on this page were active at the time of publication. The publisher is not responsible for websites that have changed their address or discontinued operation since the date of publication. The publisher reviews and updates the websites each time the book is reprinted.

Index

Numbers in ***bold italic*** refer to captions.

Individuals with Disabilities Education
Act, *41*, 43
See also legislation
insurance companies, 13
internships, *26*, 27, 29, 30, 47, 51, 56
See also education
intervention (occupational therapy
process), 11–12
interview, 49–51, 53–57

legislation, 25, *41*, 42, 43–44
licensing, 26, 27, 31–32, 34, 47
See also education

measuring outcomes (occupational therapy process), 12–13
Medicare, 43
mental hygiene movement, 36, 40–41
mobility, 6, *11*, 15
moral treatment movement, 36, 39, 45

National Board for Certification of
Occupational Therapists (NBCOT),
27, 29, 30–31, 34, 47
National Society for the Promotion of
Occupational Therapy, 40, 42
See also American Occupational
Therapy Association
neurasthenia, 36, 40
neuroanatomy, 26, 29
nursing homes, 17, 20, 22, 38, 47

occupational therapists
and career growth, 17, 37–38, 47,
56–57
and creativity, 11, 24, *46*, 51, 53
definition of, *6*, 8–9, 14
and differences of, from physical therapy, 14–15, 19
and education, 26, 27–35, 47, 50
and history of career, 39–45
and internships, *26*, 27, 29, 30, 47,
51, 56
job duties of, 7, 8–9, 11–15, 18, 19–25
and licensing, 26, 27, 31–32, 34, 47
number of, 17, 37–38, 43
personal experiences of, 10, 49–51,
53–57

and personal traits, 12, 55
physical fitness of, 18, 34–35
and process of work, 9, 11–13
salaries of, 38–39, 43
and sensory processing disorder, 6, 13
and work environments, 17–25,
38–39, 47
occupational therapy assistants (OTAs),
34, 57
"occupations," *6*, 8, 36, 37, 47
outpatient clinics, 17, 20, 24, 39, 47

physical therapy, 14–15, 19, *48*
Pinel, Philippe, 39
process of work, occupational therapy, 9,
11–13
prosthetic limbs, 54–55

reasonable accommodations, 16, 24–25, 44
See also accommodations
reconstruction aides, 41–42
Rehabilitation Act of 1973, 43
See also legislation
rehabilitation centers, 17, 22, 38, 47
research projects, 15, 25, 35, 45, 57
Rush, Benjamin, 39, 40

salaries, occupational therapist, 34,
38–39, 43
schools, 17, 23, 39, 43
sensory processing disorder, 6, 13, 23
skilled nursing facilities, 20, 22–23, 38,
47
Slagle, Eleanor Clarke, 40–41
Soldier's Rehabilitation Act, 42
See also legislation

technology, 44, 54
Technology-Related Assistance for
Individuals with Disabilities Act, 44
Tuke, William, 39

Walter Reed Hospital, 41–42
Walton, Ruth, 10, 49–57
World War I, 41–42
World War II, 42–43

York Retreat, 39

About the Author

Jennifer Hunsaker grew up wanting to become a pediatric surgeon specializing in cleft palate repair. Instead, she earned a Bachelor's Degree in Communicative Disorders and a Master's Degree in Human Resource Management and went on to work as a consultant for small businesses. Unsatisfied by the business world, she returned to her first love as a writer of medically-related content geared toward children, students, and those who work with them. When she isn't writing, she is chasing her husband, four children, and Yorkie named Wookie through the mountains of Northern Utah.